*I'm Dreaming of a
Shite Christmas*

R. J. CLARKE

I'm Dreaming of a Shite Christmas

A FESTIVE GUIDE TO OVERCOOKED SPROUTS, CHARADES AND GIBLETS

BOXTREE

First published 2006 by Boxtree
an imprint of Pan Macmillan Ltd
Pan Macmillan, 20 New Wharf Road, London N1 9RR
Basingstoke and Oxford
Associated companies throughout the world
www.panmacmillan.com

ISBN-13: 978-0752-22626-2
ISBN-10: 0-7522-2626-6

Photographic Acknowledgements (by page)
Corbis – 30, 56, 76. Getty Images – 3, 5, 7, 12, 15, 19, 31, 37, 45, 52, 68, 83, 85.
Popperfoto – 11, 32, 33, 39, 60, 64, 67, 75. Rex Features/Roger-Viollet – 18.

1 3 5 7 9 8 6 4 2

A CIP catalogue record for this book is available from
the British Library.

Printed and bound in Great Britain by
Mackays of Chatham plc, Chatham, Kent

For Ness

with thanks for the notebook,

pen and firework last Christmas

Settle back in the armchair, charge your glass, throw another roll of gift-wrap on the fire and remember to ditch your paper hat before you go to the pub. Yes, it's here again, Christmas, a time of joy, goodwill and stress in increasingly uneven measure. Still, you get time off work and they suspend the roadworks until the New Year, so it's all worth it.

Remember, it's for the kids, really. In which case, let's phase out sprouts and Christmas pudding and all have chips and jelly instead. Sprouts just stink the place out. Beforehand and afterwards.

Anyway, I hope the following festive A–Z might provide some mild amusement over the Christmas period. If not, ask whoever gave it to you if they kept the receipt.

Merry Christmas.

R. J. Clarke

Abi Titmuss (And A Happy New Year)

(*See* **Christmas Cards, Homemade**)

Advent Calendars

There are millions of advent calendars to choose from (*see* **Choices**) but there are three rules that can assist the novice. Firstly, ensure the calendar has chocolate treats behind each door. Having only an illustration of a candle or a robin behind the door just simply won't do. Secondly, ensure the calendar doesn't short-change you with only twenty-four doors instead of the full twenty-five. The final door should be a 'double door' (or 'twindow').

Doors should be opened fairly and in rotation by all members of the family but a simple calculation can ensure you always know which door to open first to end up with the 'twindow' chocolate:

$$F2\,\beta^{5}\!/_{u3}/\!\pm Q = (Rs_9) \therefore = \beta^{1}\!/_{8} \rightarrow 6 \geq {}_{SUB}25\varphi_3 0 = 4$$

where Q = members of family

Alternatively, and particularly where children are involved, it may be necessary to fractionally re-position the advent calendar on December 24th, to ensure the twindows are just out of reach.

Alphabetti-Spaghetti

A particularly impressive noodle-doodle on a Christmas card (*see **Noodle-Doodle***).

Annuals

There is no doubt that a hardback annual of a favourite comic makes for a tremendous present (*see **Gifts, Thoughtless***). However, children today seem unaware that nonchalantly adding this item towards the bottom of page 17 of their Christmas list can have long-lasting repercussions. Actively suggesting an annual can quickly lead to a serious habit – thoughtless relatives are particularly vulnerable members of society and they will soon seize on the annual present idea, making it an annual present that you will still be receiving well into your forties.

Requesting an annual is for life, not just for Christmas.

April

Trevor Bunson of Norwich finishes putting his festive Christmas lights back in the loft (*see **Christmas Lights, Exterior***).

🎄 🎄 🎄 🎄 🎄 🎄 🎄 🎄 🎄 🎄 🎄 🎄 🎄 🎄 🎄 🎄 🎄

'Bang!'

No Christmas cracker is complete without the 'bang' noise, created by two strips of cardboard and a 'banger' thing. In 1996, no fewer than 130,000 boxes of imported 'Top Luxury Best Crackers' exploded in a distribution centre in Dartford and were later found to have contained the notoriously unstable chemical component Neutrillium B5 in the 'banger'. The cloud of toxic smoke, from melted plastic novelties, could be seen from Finland as the fire raged for three days, fuelled largely by the flame-retardant paper hats (*see Yi Ylang Ylang and Paper Hats*).

The bang from the cracker was followed by a series of loud thuds as she took leave of the table via the open window – miraculously keeping her grip on the small orange plastic yo-yo – down all three flights.

Bank Account

Christmas is a time when your bank account gets a proper hammering. By using feng shui techniques from the Mystic East we can take steps to redress this imbalance in a rather pointless effort to harmonise our yin and yang (*don't see* **Yi Ylang Ylang**).

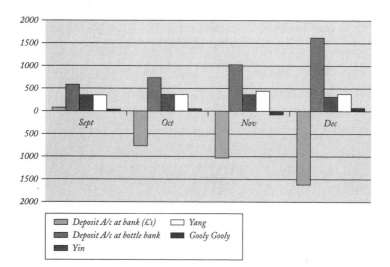

For every withdrawal made, simply increase the contributions to your deposit account at the bottle bank.

Bargains

There are no bargains before Christmas – only after Christmas, in what the retail industry calls 'Sales', where you will find all the presents you bought at half price or less.

Buying the train set from the car–boot sale had been inspired, but with only five pieces of track in the box, constructing some of the more complex layouts was to prove a challenge.

Batteries

Every toy needs batteries. Remember this.

Every toy will use up batteries by 10 o'clock on Christmas morning. You know that. So you will have thoughtfully purchased, in advance, every shape and size of spare.

Apart from those now required.

Taking the batteries out of your TV remote is a common solution but these will also be the wrong size and the TV channel will inevitably be stuck on an old episode of *Birds of a Feather*.

Baubles

In the 1950s, decorating the Christmas tree was a family activity – a time of innocence, steam trains, footballs with laces, hats, gramophones, lard, Audrey Hepburn, Brylcreem and shillings, when everybody smoked a pipe and spoke like the Queen. A time when we remained blissfully unaware of Wizzard's 'I Wish it Could be Christmas Every Day' and the dangers known today as 'bauble malfunctions'.

Christmas bauble-related accidents account for nearly 94 per cent of all injuries sustained with a Christmas bauble. They are increasingly commonplace and will almost certainly occur if basic precautions aren't followed. Always wear safety goggles. This will prevent those fiddly wire spring bits (the 'foyles') that hook over the branch and then through the gap in the top of the bauble cover (the 'ottakar') from pinging up at high speed and taking your eye out. Always wear sturdy covered shoes (not sandals . . . you hippy) to prevent glass shards from entering your foot when a bauble is dropped from a height and shatters spectacularly to a chorus of cheers and ironic clapping.

With the final bauble he had become complacent, and they knew a malfunction was only seconds away . . .

Blocked Toilets

(*See Eat Me Dates*)

Blue Peter

The lighting of the fourth and final candle on the *Blue*

Peter advent crown (made out of two coat-hangers and some flameproof tinsel) is a traditional televisual landmark, highlighting the exact moment that panic buying can begin.

Board Games

Two of the most popular board games played at Christmas are Trivial Pursuit and Monopoly. Both share one thing in common. Apart from dice. And a board. And the fact that there are loads of different 'limited editions' now. Like the 'Nottingham Forest Edition' of Monopoly or the 'Monopoly Edition' of Trivial Pursuit.

Anyway, the thing I was thinking of was that like a premium-rate phone call, they can last for hours. And it can take forever trying to land in the middle of the Trivial Pursuit board, even assuming you haven't already cheated by adding a couple of coloured 'cheeses' or 'pies' (*see **Trivial Pursuit, 'Pies'; Trivial Pursuit, 'Cheeses'; Cake and Wedge***) into your playing piece whilst *50 Favourite Wealthiest Celebrity Noddys* was on the telly. Save time by not getting Nan to ask any questions. Or answer any. Or by reading out the answer 'accidently'. By around 5 p.m. on December 28th you'll have played so often you'll be resorting to reading out the answer and guessing the question. If all else fails, try wrapping up an opponent's playing piece (including any 'cheeses' or 'pies') in a discarded Quality Street wrapper and waiting for somebody to eat it.

A similar problem in Monopoly – it takes ages to bankrupt the last player. All the other people who started playing went to the pub four hours ago. And have come back. And gone out again. Agreeing a time limit before embarking on any game of Monopoly is a good idea. Try seven minutes.

Boxing Day

When planning a wedding, a decision has to be made as to which relatives are invited to share 'the whole day' and which are invited just for the 'evening reception and finger buffet'. The result of this natural and perfectly understandable selection process, is the slightly delicate matter of having divided your entire family into two groups, or 'Premier League' relations and 'Pontin's Holidays Insurance League Division 3 (South)' relations.

Boxing Day is a perfect opportunity to meet up with 'Pontin's Holidays Insurance League Division 3 (South)' relations or, if this whole exercise of deciding the 'chavs' from the 'chav nots' leaves you feeling awkward and uneasy, to go to the races.

Brandy Butter

By taking something familiar and adding fortified wine, brandy butter is the dairy world's equivalent to alcopops. Available shortly, from larger supermarkets, will be a new brandy margarine, 'I Can't Believe It's Not Brandy Butter', despite concerns that this may lead to a spread in binge spreading. Your morning toast will become a real 'toast' if you mix this fortified spread with whisky marmalade. Cheers!

'Breast Or Thigh?'

(*See Table Manners*)

'Breast, Thigh Or Giblets?'

So those ornamental table decorations in the shape of cannonballs won't be ornamental table decorations then. They'll be the Brussels sprouts.

Brussels Sprouts

Allow to boil and then simmer gently. To ensure the correct texture these should be put on the stove no later than December 8th.

Brussels Sprouts, 'Multi-ball'

Because the amount of food prepared for Christmas dinner will always exceed the available space on plates, it

Uncle Charlie guesses 'Cat on a Hot Tin Roof', unaware the game of charades had finished a while ago. Nan was simply experiencing the inevitable after-effects of her Brussels sprouts 'Multi-ball'.

is quite common to also have dishes containing the spare vegetables on the dining table – for 'second helpings'. And so, without your prior knowledge or consent, the merest fraction of plate area that becomes uncovered is swiftly replenished with an enormous heaped spoonful of increasingly unwanted 'second helpings'.

This may begin as a welcome intrusion on your Christmas meal, especially if the giblets have been served

Just as it was being established that the lingerie he'd bought her didn't fit, their neighbours popped round for mulled wine.

and the turkey is drier than Death Valley. However, in the not altogether unlikely circumstance that the second, third, fourth and fifth helpings, magically appearing on your plate, are all Brussels sprouts, then you are experiencing a Brussels sprouts 'Multi-ball'. Resist temptation to 'tilt' table but use elbows as 'nudgers' or 'flippers' to try and stop more sprouts arriving.

Buygration

This naturally occurring annual phenomenon begins with massive numbers of wandering males congregating in lingerie departments between early December and about 4.30 p.m. on the 24th, with the sole intention of purchasing something skimpy in red and black and in a size almost-exactly-the-same-as-the-shop-assistant-only-perhaps-a-bit-larger. The item purchased will wait about a week before embarking on the arduous journey back, eventually returning to the very store from whence it came (*see Keep Your Receipt*).

Cake

(*See Trivial Pursuit, 'Pies' or throw again*)

Camping Out (for January Sales)

Watch out for the annual TV interview with the person who has spent Christmas forming a queue for the sales. The interview is often used to 'blood' a newsroom rookie. They must avoid asking the queue-header 'How long have you been queuing?' and 'What are you hoping to buy?' and for bonus points, finish each question by mouthing (to camera) 'You sad git.'

And if you're thinking of getting in there first, you're too late. Arthur Portcullis from Gateshead is there already. (Though he always leaves his camp-bed for twenty minutes around 3 a.m. to empty the wee from his Thermos flask.)

Carol Singers

Be on your guard for these seasonal 'chancers' usually comprising three or four hoodie-wearing teenagers with attitude and spots on the hunt for some free money. You'll recognise them from a couple of months ago when they were 'trick or treating'.

Sort out the Aled Joneses from the Asbo Joneses by requesting all twenty-seven verses of 'O Little Town of Bethlehem' and insisting on full backing harmonies for the chorus of 'Ding Dong Merrily on High', before bidding them farewell with your good tidings and a small selection of foreign coins.

Carpet

If you ever want to buy carpet, wait for December 26th. The same goes for beds, sofas and indeed furniture in general. And if you don't, and you've seen *Zulu*, you might as well turn the telly off on Boxing Day.

Carving The Turkey

Some things will always be 'man's work'. Like barbecues. It may be some primeval instinct, but the combination of a small fire, a few cans of lager, the smell of smoke,

Father neatly carves the turkey . . . and three inches off the dining room table.

burning fat and black charcoal seem to inspire a man, and provide the first indications that the turkey is about to be served on the 'well-done' side.

Celebrity Keep-Fit Videos

The very first celebrity keep-fit video was released in December 1979 on VHS and Betamax formats. Starring the actor who played that Charlie Hungerford from BBC1's popular detective series *Bergerac*, the video went on to sell nearly 20,000 copies and saw spin-off sales in golfing leisurewear and White Elm cigars. Last Christmas, an average of 1 in 8 households received a celebrity keep-fit video on Christmas Day. 7 out of 8 of those recipients burnt an average of 700 calories taking the unopened box back to the shop for a refund.

Charades

Parlour game experts in Halifax have calculated that the combination of alcohol, satsumas, close proximity to elderly relations, wearing a paper party hat and boredom heighten the chances of a game of charades to 40,000 to 1.

Charades has been played since Victorian times and is more popular now than ever, probably because of the massive influx of paper party hats contained within imported 'Top Luxury Best Crackers' (*see* **Yi Ylang Ylang**).

No amount of alcohol can prepare you for the shouting, gesturing, screaming, arguing and gesticulating that arise from trying to divide the room into two teams. Just make sure Nan's on their side. And if you get '*Blazing Saddles*' then it's because the game has gone on too long.

Children

'Christmas is for the children.' Repeat this ten times when you're trying to park at the supermarket on Christmas Eve because you've forgotten the cranberry sauce.

Children, Ungrateful

Maybe it's the pile of presents towering over the tree that overwhelms them but, annoyingly, small children can often appear more excited by the gift wrap than by the actual present itself.

Child behaviour expert Trixie 'Megananny' Watkins overcomes this potentially infuriating dilemma by wearing sensible outdoor shoes and by wrapping up some gift wrap in gift wrap and then seeing how they like it.

And with their stockings up, the children were now all set for the arrival of Father Christmas. It was December 3rd.

Receiving a model coach and building blocks instead of the 42-inch plasma TV had escalated into a full-blown hostage situation.

Chocolates

A safe bet Christmas gift for your nan, office colleagues (*see* **Secret Santa**), next-door neighbours, the paperboy, the Inland Revenue, the Deputy Chief Inspector, the Chief Magistrate, your solicitor, both witnesses and key members of the jury.

However, to really make an impression, wave goodbye to the industrial-sized metal tins of assorted milk chocolates from the cash and carry and head for the smaller boxes featuring soft-focus photography and words such as 'Belgian', 'Luxury', 'Continental' and 'Connoisseur'. Then study the depth of the box to establish if there is more than one layer or 'stratum'. Remember, if there is a double stratum ('strata-various'), it is illegal under Section 9 (sub section After Eight) of the 1924 Order of Consumption: Chocolatey Products (Boxed), to start on the secondary layer before all chocolate items on the primary layer have been eaten.

Chocolates, Rummaging Around For

Nobody knows who is responsible but every year somebody puts empty wrappers back in the box of Quality Street. This creates those unseemly and awkward moments spent rummaging around feeling for a solid object (*see* **Blocked Toilets**). Special Branch detectives believe the same person may also be responsible for leaving the empty envelopes in the box of After Eight mints.

Choices

Whilst we all take decisions and make choices every day of our lives, at Christmas time this natural ability can desert us.

Suddenly, deciding whether to buy Nan another foot spa or a CD (*The Best Thrash Metal Anthems in the World Ever 2*) can become overly taxing. Worse still is when the differences between two items are not immediately apparent but nevertheless significant (*see **Batteries***).

The Society for Less Choice believes the reason is because nowadays, there is just too much stuff to choose from. Spokesperson Clementine Satsuma-Mandarin says, 'The problem peaks at Christmas although there are other peak times, too, making it hard to say exactly but if I had to choose it would probably be Christmas but don't quote me on that because it might not be.'

Christmas Bonus

(*See your boss*)

❦

Christmas Cake

The only clue that a cake is homemade rather than shop-bought is that the icing will take your fillings out.

RECIPE FOR TRADITIONAL CHRISTMAS CAKE

Serves: 6–8   Preparation Time: 3 days.

You will need:
8 oz butter
4 eggs
1½ cups of sugar
1½ cups of currants, raisins and mixed fruit
1 teaspoon of cinnamon
Some icing
1 bottle of brandy
An internet account with an online supermarket

Method: Preheat oven to 300°F. Grease round a large baking tin and beat the eggs, butter and sugar until thick and creamy. Add everything else and ¼ teaspoon of brandy. Leave in prominent position as if it's a 'work-in-progress' whilst you log on to Internet and order a Luxury Christmas Cake that serves 6–8. Drain rest of brandy into glass.

Christmas Cards, Homemade

Fine for children – and the glitter industry relies on it (*see* **Glitter**) – but not advised for older members of the family.

Attempting to make a humorous homemade card, Gerry Underwood of Finchley required a picture of celebrity topless glamour model Abi Titmuss (and a Happy New Year). His search of the Internet resulted in a Home Computer Explosion all of his own (*see* **Christmas Cards, Letters Inside**).

Christmas Cards, Letters Inside

This is a fairly recent trend but is growing in popularity since the Home Computer Explosion. [*Editor's Note: Not the home computer explosion in Finchley.*]

Rather than write a simple festive greeting and a personal note, the preference is for a generic 'cover-all' letter that is typed once, printed fifty times and inserted in all cards to create an impersonal and tedious account of the previous twelve months since their last generic letter landed on your doormat. No matter that these cards are being sent to business colleagues, grandparents and the paperboy, the marvel of the generic letter is that it contains nothing for everyone. They are written in the third person and an example of a standard opening sentence is:

It's been a good year for the Harpers with the addition of our third grandchild, Hilary Jessica, a Mediterranean cruise in March and fabulous new carpets throughout (swirls and small diamonds in Sienna Beige and Burnt Aubergine in a majestic deep pile twist) . . .

[A generic Christmas Card Letter program is now available on Microsoft Windows 2000.]

🎄 *Festive Focus on:*

Christmas Eve

Every Christmas Eve morning brings with it a sense of wonder, hushed anticipation and kids maxing out on excitement and E-numbers in equally generous measures. Everything is set for the following day. The stockings are up, the presents wrapped and under the tree (and now covered with a light dusting of pine needles), the beer is cooling and the aroma of Brussels sprouts gently simmering on the stove permeates through every room. As indeed it has done for some days now. And then, the sound of the post arrives. A sense of pure fear snuffs out all earlier feelings of bonhomie. Sweat beads unattractively on your upper lip, your mouth dries and panic sets in. You're thinking 'Please let it just be the enormous electricity bill (*see* **Christmas Lights, Exterior**), applications for Platinum Credit Cards, Loans (subject to status) and that letter about the *Reader's Digest* Prize Draw' (*see* **Santa, a.k.a. Father Christmas**). Deep down you know you won't be that lucky. Sure, you'll receive all that in the post but you'll get something else too. Something you fear. Something you always get every Christmas Eve . . .

A Christmas card.

Always just one. A late arrival to add to the many that already adorn every flat surface and have already started to curl because the central heating is on too high. But this Christmas card is special. This one can be singled out, no matter how hard you try to hide it behind the others. This one will stand out like the *Blue Peter* Christmas Appeal Totaliser. This card will draw the eye more than your 480 'Multifunction Snowflake and Icicle' festive exterior lights.

Because it'll be from somebody you haven't sent one to.

You forgot them.

And it's too late to do a thing about it.

The sender may be your neighbour or somebody who only lives around the corner, but it's irrelevant. You cannot return the festive greeting without it looking totally obvious you had forgotten them. Which, of course, you had.

They know it. You know it.

They'll never send you another card and will spend Christmas wondering what they did to upset you.

You'll spend Christmas with that eggy feeling of guilt. The damage is done. Deal with it the only way you can. Check the sprouts and crack open a beer.

Christmas (Is Late This Year)

Familiar expression often used by retail analysts to explain poor sales on the High Street. Actually, I think you'll find Christmas is always on the 25th December. And if it is 'late' then will somebody tell Next they needn't put their Christmas cards out until July.

Christmas Lights, Exterior

Not so long ago the charming, whimsical idea of decorating one's home with festive lights would amuse small children and adults alike. But now seemingly every house in every street is increasingly covered with festive illuminations presumably purchased in the sales the previous Christmas.

Good-natured neighbourhood competitions take place to see who can cram the most lights onto their house. The *Guinness Book of Records* currently recognises number 62 Arunhurst Drive in Norwich as the house with the most Christmas decorations.

Owner Trevor Bunson started his collection of illuminated novelty lights with one flashing Rudolph in 1975. Since then it has grown to such an extent that during the Christmas holiday period, 62 Arunhurst Drive can be seen from space and switching on all the lights causes a power surge in the National Grid equivalent to turning on

48,793 assorted Christmas decorations in one go. Pride of place is the 8-metre tall, 'Multifunction Flash 'n' Synchro-Strobe Santa with Sleigh Combo' which adds festive cheer to the community and £1,350 to the Bunson electricity bill (*see Fig. 1, not **Figgy Pudding**).

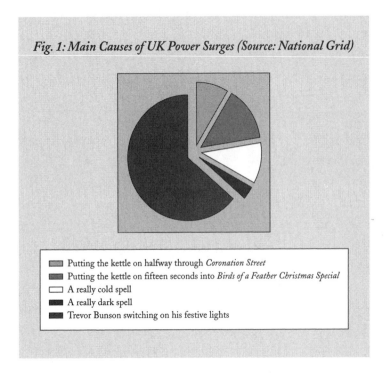

Fig. 1: Main Causes of UK Power Surges (Source: National Grid)

Putting the kettle on halfway through *Coronation Street*
Putting the kettle on fifteen seconds into *Birds of a Feather Christmas Special*
A really cold spell
A really dark spell
Trevor Bunson switching on his festive lights

Christmas Lights, Interior

In the UK, there have been fewer than sixty-eight recorded incidents of last year's Christmas lights working first time. Many frustrating hours can be wasted 'bulb-twizzling' in an effort to make the lights work, and it is a cause of colourful language and telephone calls to B&Q and The Samaritans.

Such has been the increase in Repetitive Strain Injuries (RSI) caused by 'bulb-twizzling', that doctors representing seven local health authorities from across the country have written to the Board of Medical and Health Practitioners recommending that the now common injury is officially recognised and given a long Latin name that'd look good on their prescriptions. A spokesman for the Board of Medical and Health Practitioners confirmed they had received seven letters and were recommending that they be typed next time so they didn't look like the scribbles of a small child.

A useful factsheet, 'My Bloody Lights Won't Work', is now available by sending a self-addressed envelope to T. Bunson, 62 Arunhurst Drive, Norwich.

Christmas Lights, Switching On The

Every major town and city in the UK will have Christmas streetlights turned on by celebrities of varying quality (*see* **Quality Street**). For example, regular shoppers on London's busy Oxford Street can usually expect a genuine 'A-lister' whereas residents of Dorking haven't recognised their 'celebrity' since 1968. But have you ever wondered who turns the lights off again?

The chances are it'll be Arthur Ferguson of Denby Avenue in Luton. Like Mike Tyson, Mr Ferguson has made a career of putting people's lights out since becoming a volunteer ARP warden back in 1945. Check out *www.xmaslightsoff.co.uk* for Arthur merchandise, photographs of towns in the dark and for the Powersave–sponsored 'Big Christmas Switch Off' tour dates.

Christmas Lists

The items that appear on a child's list for Father Christmas have changed a little over the last few decades. Old favourites like a piece of orange, a spinning top and a marble have been replaced with a new PlayStation, DVD player, iPod, this week's Man Utd home-strip, sunglasses, a new pair of jeans, a motorbike, an upgraded mobile phone, trainers, jewellery, the *Beano Annual* and some cash.

The findings have been identified by temporary seasonal staff working for the Royal Mail whose job it is to open all letters addressed to 'Father Christmas, Lapland', looking for a return address and any money.

'A dolly? Get real! I'm not leaving without a pair of Jimmy Choos and a portable DVD player.'

Christmas Logs
(*See **Christmas Number 2s***)

Christmas Number 1s

Do we really care who is number 1 in the Hit Parade at Christmas? Are we interested to know who is number 1? Ever? In the old days when you had proper singers and beat combos and songs you could dance to, we cared. But now? Who gives a Christmas number 2?

Christmas Number 2s

(*See* **Brussels Sprouts**, **Eat Me Dates**, *a man about a dog and, somewhat inevitably,* **Blocked Toilets**)

Christmas Presents, Hiding Places For

It's a fact that children will always find where their Christmas presents are hidden. Child behaviour expert

'I found this crap on top of your wardrobe – you can take them all back and I'll have money instead.'

Trixie 'Megananny' Watkins suggests tackling this annoying habit by 'double-bluffing' and leaving their presents unwrapped and on full view and then seeing how they like it.

Christmas Presents, Unexpected

An unexpected Christmas gift always means so much more (*see photo below*).

Christmas Presents, Unexploded

(*See photo above*)

Christmas Pudding

Placing a sixpence inside the pudding and then microwaving on full power allows the coin to experience similar temperatures to that of the Space Shuttle re-entering the earth's atmosphere.

650 watt (Category B)	15 minutes
750 watt (Category D)	10 minutes
850 watt (Category E)	8 minutes 15 seconds

(All appliances vary, these are guidelines only.)

The mystery of the 'extra' sixpence and the 'missing' watch battery was about to be solved.

Christmas Specials

The highest recorded viewing audience for a TV Christmas Special was the 1983 feature-length action-adventure starring the A Team.

The episode, 'Quit your jibber jabba – it's Christmas, fool' was seen by over 23 million viewers when it was shown by mistake during the half-time break of the FA Cup Final. The incident went on to form the basis of *Sunday Times* non-fiction bestseller *Telephone Exchange Meltdown*.

Christmas Stamps, Overbuying

However tempting, resist bulk-buying Christmas stamps. The post office never run out and whilst buying loads will save having to re-join that mile-long queue of grannies, it is an offence, under the 1967 Post Office Festive Stamps Act, to use them beyond January 7th.

🛷 *Festive Focus on:*

Christmas Tree, Selection Of

Standing in the pub car park choosing your tree in the persistent drizzle is a seasonal highlight, signalling the beginning of the Christmas festivities. Resisting the temptation to start the aforementioned festivities too early is always a good discipline. Any tree bought before midday on December 6th will be bald by Christmas Eve but for half a dozen stubborn orangey-brown needles that have yet to join the quarter of a million or so that are already embedded in the carpet. And no amount of tinsel can disguise that fact (*see **Needles, Pine***).

And I don't believe you ever got a receipt for that tree did you? Funny that (*see **Keep Your Receipt***).

Selecting the correct height of tree is made easier by following the procedure below. (Note: The following instructions must be followed in sequence.)

Getting Started

Step 1. Measure the space.
Step 2. Buy tree to fit space previously measured in Step 1.

Cont. overleaf

35

Appendix 1

Always take into account that any bucket/stand/bucket of sand that you put the tree in will add just enough height to make it too tall for the space.

Troubleshooting

Tree too big for space?/ Tree doesn't fit space?/ Space too small for tree?

Solutions:

(i) Saw off top of tree.

(ii) Saw off bottom of tree.

Both troubleshooting options (as described in Appendix 1) are best tackled outside. In the persistent drizzle that has now become more of a heavy downpour. It may help to know that this common oversight has been a part of Christmas since Victorian times, as this 1840s traditional playground rhyme reveals:

> *Abstain 'til the 6th with all yore might,*
> *Lo! Measure the room to establish ye height.*
> *Alloweth for a buckett or it could go scarey . . .*
> *. . . Furtively sawing the legs off the fairie*

Nipping down to the park to lop 3ft off a tree provided a great low-cost afternoon out for the kids.

Christmas Trees, Recycling

Do your bit for the enviroment. An average five-foot Christmas tree provides enough bark, sap, pine needles and general tree debris to fill an average family hatchback.

So don't mess up your car, ask your council to collect it. Or else it'll stay on the pavement with all the others.

Chrome Effect

How often does a bloke request something in 'chrome effect'? Yet come Christmas, all those little gift items for men appear and they're always in 'chrome effect': tie-racks, coin sorters, personal grooming kits, hip flasks, alarm clocks, tax disc holders, business card holders, gear knobs and so on. Based on current usage, scientists predict that, by 2057 we will have run out of chrome effect and may have to resort to using real chrome.

Cold Turkey

in a sandwich with a spot of cranberry sauce helps avoids waste. Getting wasted can result in a spot of cold turkey with no sauce. Don't get them mixed up.

Compilation Album

(*See* **Now That's What I Call Music** *and* **Repeat-fest**)

Crossword Puzzles

At Christmas, these suddenly quadruple in size. Why? Nobody knows and it remains a puzzle.

Decorations, Taking Down

(*See* **Twelfth Night**)

Discovering Santa Doesn't Exist

You'll always remember where you were when you discovered Santa was actually the brainchild of a well-known soft drinks company.

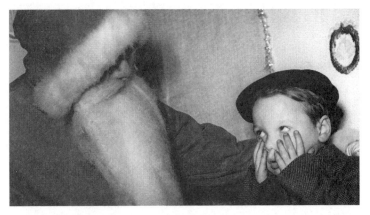

The terrible realisation that behind the false beard and smell of Old Holborn it was unmistakably Mr Jarvis from the off-licence.

Drinking, How Early Can You Start?

If you're concerned you may be 'starting a bit early' on Christmas morning, simply set your alarm to go off ten minutes later.

Droning

(*See **Male Relatives, Unfunny***)

Droning On and On

(*See **Male Relatives, Still Unfunny Three Hours Later***)

Dustbin Day

We are all aware the refuse collection day changes during the holiday period. This much we do know. It's to do with all the Bank Holidays. At some point, we face having to guess when to next put our rubbish out for the dustmen. Deciphering experts at Bletchley Park using an Enigma machine have failed to crack the secret 'collection-day-cycle-rota-code-matrix', believed to originate from a temperature-controlled bunker underneath county council offices in Plymouth.

Householders are faced with a staggering 23 million possible permutations of when their next collection day will be, rising to 47 billion if Christmas Day falls on a Tuesday.

E-Mails

Attached to that 'hilarious' e-mail of the dancing cartoon Father Christmas that froze your office computer for twenty-five minutes while it downloaded, will be at least four of the biggest viruses known to man. They will lay dormant for weeks . . . until just before you click 'save' on that fiendishly complicated spreadsheet you've been working on for the previous five hours.

Just as well you didn't forward that e-mail to all your mates then.

Easter Eggs

On sale at Woolworths December 26th. Hot Cross Buns available at Tesco the following day.

Eat Me Dates

Always be suspicious of a festive food that contains, in its title, an instruction. This indicates – usually with good reason – that there is room for a degree of confusion. We don't have 'Eat Me Mince Pies' or 'Drink Me Beer' because we recognise these products as something we would eat or drink. Close scrutiny of the Eat Me Dates will reveal where the confusion lies (*see **Blocked Toilets***).

Eurovision Christmas Song Contest

This seasonal spin-off from the Eurovision Song Contest has, amusingly, yet to be won by Turkey. Last year's UK entry 'Snowy Snowy Snow (It's Snowy)' by Fabreeze finished in joint twenty-ninth place. It's easy to forget that Wizzard's 'I Wish It Could Be Christmas Every Day' was an entry in the 1973 contest, finishing second to last and 426 points behind winners Luxembourg. Billionaire Roy Wood from Wizzard, speaking from his luxury penthouse suite in Dubai said, 'I'd forgotten all about that.'

Father Christmas, Leaving Things Out For

Leaving mince pies, a small sherry and carrots for the reindeer is a tradition that recently has faced increasing opposition from the Anti-Drink Drive lobby. Meanwhile, pressure groups working on behalf of the UK's dads have campaigned for a gradual phasing out of the carrots and mince pie in exchange for upgrading the small sherry to a large one, and for the introduction of a porno mag.

'Fifty Greatest'

Christmas telly becomes swamped with 'compilation' shows, hosted by excitable 'D-listers', which are a marvellous opportunity to re-show us old stuff while producers of new programmes are getting hammered at the office party. Examples include *50 Greatest TV Detectives*, *50 Greatest TV Sitcoms* and *50 Greatest Celebrity Haircuts*. Listen out to be excitedly told 'after the break, we'll count down numbers 37 to 28, as voted by you!'

Work has already started on *50 Greatest 50 Greatest Compilations*.

Until then, settle back and enjoy *Another 50 Greatest Embarrassing Celebrity TV Blooper Sitcom Haircuts*. As voted by you.

Figgy Pudding

There's plenty left, top shelf at the back of the fridge.

What do you mean we didn't buy any?

Figgies are actually small animals belonging to the Hamster family. As a result, Paul Hamster is on the UK Rich List at number 16.

But what the hell are giblets? Anybody? (*See* **Giblets**.)

Foot Spas

The annual UK appearance of foot spas coincides with that of the brambling, a small bird similar to a chaffinch. Both appear on these shores in great numbers every year, always at Christmas time and have usually disappeared again by New Year though the occasional straggler can be spotted as late as mid-January. Bill Oddie and a BBC film crew are currently on location in southern Europe to investigate similarities in their migratory patterns. It might even be worth considering paying your TV licence fee to ensure they stay out there.

Each year, many foot spas return to the same location, and incredibly, even the same branch. Usually Currys or Dixons.

(*See also* **Keep Your Receipt** *and* **Unwanted Presents**).

Fresh or Frozen?

(*See* **Turkey, Ordering**) If electing for a fresh bird, always instruct your butcher that you require a turkey 'so fresh it was making plans for the weekend'.

Giblets

What the hell are giblets anyway? They are located inside your Christmas turkey in a small plastic bag. That's probably what killed it.

'Nice one, Nan – I can see that bag of giblets looks done to a turn.'

Gift Tag

Your free cut out 'n' keep gift tag.

Gifts, Thoughtless

Retailers these days cater for our every Christmas gift need – no matter now thoughtless we are. Not long ago, receiving a pair of socks and a mug could be perceived as a couple of rather thoughtless presents. Now, thanks to a brilliant marketing initiative aimed specifically at the 'thoughtless gifter' (demographic: T/G1s), a range of merchandise is available from larger department stores. The range consists of 'boxed-sets', each comprising a mug *and* a pair of socks.

Andy Reddle-Jessop at top marketing agency KC&P Creative explains: 'We wanted something that would tick all the boxes, so, thinking outside the box, we hit on the concept of putting them inside a box.'

*(See also **Now That's What I Call Music; Annuals; Novelty Slippers/Socks/Ties; Presents, Makeweight; Git, Thoughtless;** etc)*

Gift Wrap

There are rules. Just because it's all foil and shine (and in a '3 for 2' offer) does not mean it'll wrap nicely. In fact they don't even fold properly. You'd be better off with the Jumbo Roll from the petrol station (*see **Sellotape** and **Children, Ungrateful***).

Git, Thoughtless

(*See **Gifts, Thoughtless***)

Glitter

Comprising billions of small glittery particles ('glitterati') with the chemical element Gti2.0, glitter is a standard component featuring on 87 per cent of all Christmas cards made by small children. Scientists are particularly interested in the adhesive properties of glitter and its ability to stick to everything and get everywhere other than where you wanted it.

Great Aunts

You'll find a Great Aunt who stays for Christmas is anything but great. Don't be disappointed.

🎄 🎄 🎄 🎄 🎄 🎄 🎄 🎄 🎄 🎄 🎄 🎄 🎄 🎄 🎄 🎄 🎄

Hangover Cures (1)

Whatever your favourite tabloid newspaper, magazine or daytime TV show they will all feature this seasonal stalwart. Gone are the days of the old herbal remedies using nettles, vinegar and owl droppings because thanks to binge drinking and, increasingly, binge spreading (*see*

Brandy Butter), hangover cures are big business and the supermarket shelves are full of them.

Whilst feature writers and Richard & Judy will sample a selection of the range and award each of them marks, do remember that they are professional media types and mixing drinks like this would give a normal person a hangover.

Hangover Cures (2)

Drunk too much? Feeling rough? Head spinning? Nauseous? Chances are you've been mixing your hangover cures. At the time of writing, there are no readily available cures for hangover cures. Try nettles, vinegar and owl droppings.

Horoscopes

> **Your Horoscope for the Year Ahead**
>
> **Will you be lucky in love? Will the New Year be a healthy, wealthy and happy one? What do the Stars have in store for you?**
>
> With Mars travelling across your relationship chart and travel planet Mercury in Gamma Quadrant, large yellowy planet Saturn is influencing your business decisions.
>
> A private matter may remain private if connected to somebody else you know so stay strong with your love destiny and luck will visit in the form of a number or letter. You are ready to make a call that will provide the expert answers you need.
>
> For a more detailed horoscope call 09800 followed by your star sign. Calls cost £2.50 per minute and go on a bit.

Icicle
(*See* '*Second Cowboy*')

Ironic Clapping
(*See* **Baubles** *and possibly* **Giblets**)

Jigsaws

What seemed like a great present at the time can quickly become the source of major family arguments. According to The Samaritans there are four common 'conflict flashpoints':

i) Not doing the edge pieces first.

ii) Not helping to search for a missing edge piece.

iii) Finding it stuck to the palm of your hand and being accused of 'saving it'.

iv) Putting it in and then tapping it four times with your finger in a self-satisfied manner.

v) Unrealistic expectations of completing before Easter.

June

The month when the Hotel Excelsior in Stoke-on-Trent put their decorations up and when Trevor Bunson of Norwich gets his festive lights down from the loft (*see* **Christmas Lights, Exterior**). This is also the month when full details of the Queen's Speech, the plot for the *Eastenders Christmas Special* and the New Year's Honours List are all revealed (*see* **New Year's Honours List**) and when BBC Radio Essex re-instate 'Mull of Kintyre' to their airplay list after a three-week break.

Jokes (in Christmas crackers)

Advances in technology have enabled experts in Denmark to begin the task of accurately carbon-dating jokes in Christmas crackers. The oldest joke discovered so far was unearthed whilst studying 30,000 imported 'Top Luxury Best Crackers' dumped in a lay-by. Dr Christian Andersson from Jacobsson's Cracker Research Laboratory in Denmark's bustling Copenhagen revealed that 'carbon-dating this particular consignment was made easier because they were all fire-damaged. The one about the National Elf Service we believe dates back to the Neolithic period. Interestingly, it wasn't funny then either.'

Keep Your Receipt

'Oooh that's nice, have you kept the receipt?'
  Enough said.

Kittens, Tips For Gift Wrapping

The reason pets make rubbish Christmas presents is that they are virtually impossible to wrap. Resist what is admittedly only a small and unlikely temptation to splash out on Luxury Gift Wrap, as a Jumbo Roll purchased with £30 worth of unleaded is easier to poke air-holes through (*see a trained therapist*).

Lapland, Christmas Trips To

Gavin McIntyre (36) of Newcastle has good reason never to forget his 'Dream Daytrip to Lapland' last Christmas. Gavin takes up the story:

> I'd always wanted to go to Lapland for Christmas ever since I was a little kiddie, but my parents were having to work all hours just to pay the electricity bill for our exterior Christmas lights. So when I got a bonus at work and was trying to decide which loan to put it towards, I spotted this 'Dream Daytrip to Lapland' advert in the back of my paper. I was a little embarrassed, being a single bloke in his mid-thirties like, so I phoned the company and they were terrific, reassuring me it was not a problem and could I just give them my credit card number please.
>
> On the day, their taxi-service arrived right on time, and we headed north towards Edinburgh. An hour later and I was sitting with my hand luggage in what I assumed was one of

those British Airways private airport lounges I'd heard about, all deep comfy chairs and soft lighting, having a drink to calm my pre-flight nerves.

It was probably after the third or fourth girl had done her routine when I called over the nearest scantily-clad waitress and explained that I was expecting to get to Lapland for a one-on-one with Santa. She told me this had been 'Lapland' since last August and she didn't know Santa but they had a Samantha and would she do?

It was the best Christmas I ever had and once I've cleared off the loan I had to take out to pay for it, I'll definitely be going again.

Last Posting Dates

Last guaranteed second-class surface and airmail postal dates for Christmas are as follows:

Destination	Last Second-Class Surface Post
Australia, Far East, South Africa, Canada, New Zealand	Two weeks ago
Mainland Europe (incl. Channel Islands), USA, Ipswich	One week ago
Mainland UK, Dogger, Fisher, German Bight, Forties, Cromarty, Sole, Lundy, Rockall, Biscay, Viking, South East Iceland, East Croydon, Clapham Junction then all stations to Harpenden	Yesterday

Loans

Need cash to pay for Christmas? Why not borrow some by applying for one of the hundreds of loans on offer from the companies towards the back of the newspaper. CCJs, Asbos, STDs? No problem. As long as you are a homeowner and your house is worth more than you need to borrow, you're in business. All you need is a microscope with 675 x magnification powers to read the small print.

Magazine Partworks

These all start at Christmas. You know the sort. Issue 1 only 99p, Issue 2 comes with Free Binder. In just 196 weekly instalments build your own 1:24 scale model of a Citroën Saxo.

Issue 1 comes complete with your first three wing-nuts, a cup-holder and some glue. Just four years later, your loft contains sixty-five complete binders and you are the proud owner of a rather gluey model car the size of a shoe – and all for just £36,876.

Male Relatives, Unfunny

What's yours called? (*See **Droning***)

Male Relatives, Still Unfunny Three Hours Later

(*See **Droning On and On** and see if you can find an excuse to leave*)

Meltdown

Banking and financial institutions have identified twenty-seven key 'industry standard' stages to describe credit card

Her father's credit card was fast approaching a 'Code 27', less than an hour after she'd found it.

use. Code 1 = 'light/occasional'. Code 27 = 'meltdown'. Approximately 87 per cent of all UK credit cards are Code 27s between December 20th–December 24th. During the same period there were just two Code 1s in the UK.

Bank fraud officials made arrests at both addresses.

Mistletoe

Kissing under the mistletoe has long been a Christmas custom but a new survey reveals the traditional snog at the office party can be fraught with embarrassing obstacles such as a punch in the face.

The poll of more than 45,000 office workers, conducted by Glossy-Buff Shoe Polish Ltd, reveals that the Top 5 most off-putting things when kissing under the mistletoe are:

1. Unpolished shoes 85%

2. Bad breath 7%

3. Moustaches (male or female) 4%

4. Another reason 3%

5. Something else 1%

Mulled Wine

Christmas is the only time of year you can get away with serving warm wine. So disposing of that bottle of Happy Shopper Beaujolais has never been easier (*see* **Snowball**).

'Must-have' Toy

Every Christmas there will be a 'must-have' toy, an item that will appear at the top of every list for Santa. It is therefore relatively straightforward to establish what the current MHT is by looking at the first item on any list for Father Christmas. The one that's underlined. Three times. In felt-tip. The one that's in capital letters.

And the one that's sold out in all the shops.

The one that's only available on eBay for £500 (*See also* **Tracy Island**)

Napkins

Over the holiday period, millions of people select festive paper table-napkins adorned with holly, robins and other seasonal motifs.

And of those millions, only about three people don't have loads left over. Look out for these Christmas napkins reappearing at summer picnics and especially at barbecues or on Bonfire Night to help get the fire started.

Nativity Play

Last year, 2,732 registered primary-school teachers left the profession, citing verbal and physical abuse as a major contributing factor in their decision. The chief source of this appalling behaviour was from parents disappointed that their child had not been given the leading role in the school nativity play.

'The temptation to give out multiple lead roles is enormous,' said one teacher who wished to remain anonymous. The tall, dark-haired female teacher (35) who teaches Year 3 pupils in her slight Geordie accent at Appledale County Primary in York continues: 'Last year we had three Josephs, four Marys and eighteen Wise Men – there just simply aren't enough leading roles to go round but we need to keep the parents off our backs. The days are gone when kids would be happy playing the role of 'a tree' or 'an icicle' in the traditional nativity plays or 'second cowboy' in the updated versions. Now all of a sudden they're all little Al Pacinos or Dame Judi Denchs and unless they have the lead role, their own dressing room, lightly chilled alcopops and their face at the top of the Souvenir Nativity Play Tea Towel, their parents come round and let our tyres down.'

Needles, Knitting

'I don't care if Nan did knit them specially, mine's going on the fire.'

Needles, Pine

Nothing beats having a real Christmas tree. It's a timeless reminder that the festive season is with us. Another reminder is treading on a pine needle with bare feet the following May. Scientists have shown that the best technique to remove a shedding tree with the minimum amount of needle-drop is by filling the bucket with petrol and setting it on fire. For a low-cost, needle-free alternative, buy a plastic tree and spray liberally with a pine-scented air freshener, located near the bleach and toilet cleaning products in all major supermarkets (*see* **Christmas Trees, Recycling** *and* **Christmas Tree, Selection Of**).

New Year's Honours List

Details are kept a closely guarded secret, under constant 24-hour armed guard, alongside details of the Queen's Speech and the plot for the double-episode Christmas special of *Eastenders*. It remains in this state until it's in all the newspapers and been on the radio and the telly.

According to *Debrett's Etiquette and Peerage* an existing Earl cannot be awarded an OBE as they would become an Ear lobe.

Noodle-Doodle

The unidentified signature on a corporate Christmas card (*see* **Alphabetti-Spaghetti**).

Novelty Slippers

The demand for these huge, unwieldy, impractical, stupid novelty-shaped slippers remains as big as ever. But only at Christmas. However, this feat of manufacturing know-how can also leave the recipient not knowing-how their feet will fit in them. Gordon Enormous, founder of Large

Slippers Ltd in Bradford admits it's a problem finding room in the more complicated designs to leave a hole for the feet. 'The hardest brief we ever had was to make some Rudolph the Reindeer novelty slippers. We made 750,000 pairs but there wasn't enough space for the antlers. Fortunately, Scooby-Doo became popular again and we shifted the lot.'

Novelty Socks

'I know! Uncle Graham likes fishing, so he'll love these haddock motif socks.'

No, actually he won't (*see* **Gifts, Thoughtless; Unwanted Presents; Panic Buying Food; Things You Wouldn't Be Seen Dead In;** *and loads more probably*).

Novelty Ties

These are for presents only. On no account should they be actually worn.

Now That's What I Call Music

Compilation CDs abound at Christmas but none cash in quite so freely on the 'thoughtless gifter' as *Now That's What I Call Music* (*NTWICM*). In amongst *The Best of*, *The Greatest Hits of*, *The Platinum Collection*, *The Singles*

Collection and *The Ultimate Hits of* is this annual compendium that is geared to the person who clearly has no idea what else to buy (*see* **Choices**). Statistics show that nearly 74 per cent of sales of *NTWICM* albums are on Christmas Eve – narrowly beating gift vouchers and humour books. It is calculated that if you put all the people who have bought *NTWICM* albums on the Isle of Wight it might not be a bad idea.

(*See also* **Gifts, Thoughtless**)

Office Party, Legal Repercussions Of

Employers and employees need to be aware of the serious legal repercussions that can follow a drunken remark over the Twiglets and warm wine at the office Christmas party. For example, a senior City lawyer was successfully sued for a reported £37 million after he described a female colleague as having 'great baps'.

To avoid the risk of similar situations, always ensure there won't be any lawyers at your Christmas party.

Overcooked Brussels Sprouts

(*See* **Blocked Toilets**)

Over-commercialisation (1)

Too many perfume adverts on TV is a clear case of over-commercialisation (*see **Perfume***).

— *He's not breathing!*
— *Shut up and search his pockets for my MP3 player.*

Over-commercialisation (2)

The worry is that the true meaning of Christmas is at risk of being lost. If we carry on like this it won't be very long before children will see December 25th as just a day when they get presents.

Panic Buying Food

From a nation of shopkeepers to a nation of shoppers. The supermarkets are going to close for one day. Maybe two. What will we eat? How will we survive? It would be like this if there was a war. Food shortages and the inevitable rationing.

To avoid this, simply buy in bulk. Everybody does it until stuff starts running out. So this forces us to buy in bulk two, three or four times. A day. Stockpiling brandy butter, cornering the market in cranberry sauce, creating a mountain of Brussels sprouts and forcing the price of parsnips on the London Stock Exchange up 67 points. Check those sell-by dates though. Bulk-buying festive foodstuff with a 'best before December 24th' is a basic mistake for the inexperienced panic-buyer.

Pantomime

A great British tradition that provides a fabulous opportunity to hoot with laughter, forget all your troubles and loudly shout, 'Who?'

Yes indeed, a poster advertising a forthcoming pantomime is guaranteed to cheer up even the most miserable soul! Without a flicker of recognition, study the 'star-studded' cast and then look for the explanation in brackets underneath e.g. 'the second prison guard in TV's *The Bill*', 'the man in the shop in episode 4 of TV's *Open All Hours*', or 'Katie in Channel 5's hospital drama show that clashes with *Eastenders*'.

A glittering TV and showbiz career? It's behind you!

Paper Hats

Advances in the paper headwear industry have ensured that no matter the size of your head, the hat won't fit. Nan's hat will slip over her mouth to become a further obstacle that the incoming heaped forkful of figgy pudding will need to negotiate.

Other hats seem small enough for Barbie to wear. As an ankle bracelet. Exchanging an ill-fitting paper hat with your neighbour is one option to consider, but do remember you still have their hedge-trimmers and by the time you get back your dinner will be cold.

Paper Hats, Fashion Tips For

Fashion expert Minkie D'Angelo predicts the big trend this season will be for 'seams to the side':

Judging from the big shows at New York, Milan and Paris, the look is teamed with a more rakish angle, low-slung to just above the right ear. Last year's 'Royal' look, where the hat was worn like a crown, is just so totally out. The colour palette is the simply timeless light aubergine, a bold lime-green and a pale orange . . . but for real pizzazz there's a divine dusky red that's simply to die for.

Milano, Italia: Models wear paper hats from the Dolce and Gabbana winter collection.

Perfume

All perfume costs 0.0001p per fl tonne. The money you actually pay is mainly for the embossed decahexoctagonal shaped glass bottle. The remainder goes towards the TV advertising campaign featuring the feather-mask-wearing couple, each holding a goldfish and sitting astride a leopard on a deserted beach (with the obligatory whispered French voice-over). The advert was shot on location in Antigua by the 764-strong film-crew and the 'deserted beach' used in the shoot was, in fact, absolutely packed until the leopard turned up.

Pets

Sensible people know that 'pets are for life and not just for Christmas' (*see* **Kittens, Tips For Gift Wrapping**).

'Yep, four house bricks should do it. Can we go to the canal now, Daddy?'

Presents (For People Who Have Everything)

(*See* **Chrome Effect**)

Presents, Inappropriate

No matter how great the temptation (sometimes referred to as 'panic'), avoid buying underwear for your in-laws. And hopefully they'll extend the same courtesy to you.

Presents, Makeweight

When it comes to buying presents, the rules clearly state that it should not be something that you would (a) buy yourself anyway and especially (b) buy yourself anyway during your weekly shop.

It therefore follows that gift wrapping a jar of marmalade / a bar of soap / shoe polish / toothpaste / pair of Marigolds or any other such item – whilst useful – does not constitute a present. Even if you use gift tags and a bow.

Presents, Uneven Number Of

During the traditional handing-out of the presents from under the tree, there is nothing more awkward than having an uneven number of gifts for each of the assembled recipients. Imagine the scene where everybody has opened all their gifts and yet a further three parcels remain . . . all for the same person and invariably a small child.

To avoid this feeling of embarrassed mortification and undue distress, it's easy to give in to temptation and buy a few makeweight items (*see **Presents, Makeweight** – it's the not very funny one above, that was put in to make **Presents, Uneven Number Of** look better*).

However, on no account should 'makeweight' presents be purchased to even things up and instead, any 'overspill' presents intended for the same small child should simply be taken back to the shops for a full refund (*see **Keep your Receipt***).

Punch

(*See **Mulled Wine; Snowball** and **Mistletoe***)

Quality Street

'Someone's had all the quality and left me with the street.' Derivation unknown but poss. wartime expression and now used when rummaging for chocolates or when being disappointed at discovering who will be switching on your town's Christmas lights (*see **Christmas Lights, Switching On The** and **Chocolates, Rummaging Around For***).

Radio-Controlled Cars

Each year at Christmas time, retailers across the country that normally sell clothes or shoes or televisions or light bulbs suddenly realise they have overlooked one key seasonal product: remote-controlled cars. Obviously.

Stored away for ten months of the year, radio-controlled cars prove a 100 per cent reliable Christmas gift line for any retailer, regardless of their normal business. Andy Reddle-Jessop at top marketing agency KC&P Creative predicts an even brighter future for radio-controlled vehicles (RCVs): 'By teaming two blue-chip seasonal sales stalwarts – namely RCVs and socks – and putting them in one big box, retailers can hit on a win-win combo. The top creatives here at KC&P believe the next 'big' thing following 'big' boxes will be radio-controlled socks.'

Repeat-fest

Technical term for a TV programme that pretends to be new but is actually a whole bunch of repeats bundled into one inexpensive 'All New' programme. The music industry call this a 'compilation album'. (*See also* **Review Of The Year** *and* **Zulu**)

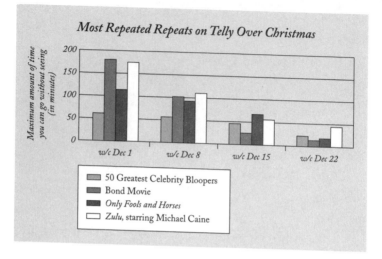

Most Repeated Repeats on Telly Over Christmas

50 Greatest Celebrity Bloopers
Bond Movie
Only Fools and Horses
Zulu, starring Michael Caine

Review of The Year

This will appear in most newspapers the day after their Christmas party. We don't actually need their recap because we were there the first time. It's what the television world would call a 'repeat'. Except they can't because they already fill hours with their own brand of repeats, just leaving small gaps in their televisual schedule for 'repeatfest' shows like *50 Favourite Sitcoms* and *Review of the Year*.

Ring Tones

Mobile phones are no longer *just* phones. Manufacturers compete to add more and more features such as Internet access, SMS text messaging, camera, hedge trimmers, a reversing light and small tumble dryer. The latest mobile from Switzerland features a bottle opener, toothpick, screwdriver, tweezers, nail file and compass. The one thing they all have in common is their ability to produce irritating ring tones. And somebody thought it would be hilarious to produce festive ring tones. So don't just expect to hear Slade hit 'Merry Xmas Everybody' in certain department stores from June 1st, now you can hear it on certain mobile phones until about May 31st. As a result, Slade front-man Noddy Holder appears on TV's *50 Favourite Wealthiest Celebrity Noddys* at No. 39.

Salmon

(Sea food starter)

Samaritans, The

*(See **Christmas Lights, Interior** and **Jigsaws**)*

Santa, a.k.a. Father Christmas

He knows if you've been good or bad. He knows what you want for Christmas. He knows when you're sleeping. He knows where you live. He knows a market research company that will pay top dollar for this information.

Santa is responsible for your junk-mail.

'Second Cowboy'

An indication that your child has failed to secure the lead in the school nativity play (*see **Nativity Play***). Coincidently, small child Ben Worthington of St Neots near Cambridge asked Santa for a cowboy outfit but was disappointed to receive a costume comprising overalls, a hardhat, builder's belt and tea mug.

'Secret Santa'

Increasingly popular in dull offices, the idea is to randomly draw the name of a work colleague from a hat and buy him or her a present for under £5. Retailers have latched on to this trend and are sourcing items specifically from specialist suppliers (*See **Yi Ylang Ylang***).

Sellotape

Beware cheap imitations. Wrapping your stuff up at 11 p.m. on Christmas Eve can be stressful enough without having the added pressure of not being able to find the end of the roll of tape. Hold up to a light-bulb to help locate the microscopically thin line that indicates the start/end point. Alternatively, try using Blu-Tack, string, or some of the left-over glue from the ongoing *Battleships of World War Two* magazine partwork project. What do you mean you've used all the glue cementing the communications mast to the aft gun turret as instructed in issue 84? Well, try not buying the 'Sellotape' from the petrol station then.

Shopping Mall Santas

You just paid £5 to visit a bloke dressed as Santa in a tent at the Arndale Centre? Police investigations are ongoing but you can expect a caution and possible community service order.

After thousands of rejections, petty-thief, stalker and WWE wrestling fan Ron Blackwood secures a position as a Shopping Mall Santa at the first attempt.

Snowball

Like giblets, mulled wine and the punch you get at Christmas (*see **Mistletoe***) nobody ever really knows what they've done to deserve them.

Spending Christmas Abroad

In recent years it has become increasingly popular to get away for Christmas (*see all other entries*).

Spoilers

There's nothing worse than knowing exactly what your present is. That's the whole point of gift wrap. Professional gift wrappers can disguise a 500 piece jigsaw as

'It's not the CD you wanted but if it doesn't fit, "Naughty Nymphos" will exchange within 28 days.'

an object that has the shape, size and weight of a 'sit-on' lawnmower.

However, every Christmas, just as you start to open your 'surprise' present, the family's 'designated spoiler' will loudly tell you exactly what it is. Merry Christmas!

Table Manners

According to *Debrett's Etiquette and Modern Manners*, Christmas dinner should be served no later than 3.26 p.m. Other essential advice includes how one should correctly pull a cracker, how to pass the cranberry sauce (mirror, signal, manoeuvre) and how a gentleman might best avoid disgrace when tackling the 'breast or thigh?' question.

Tea Towels

Storming towards the top of the FTSE 100 leader board following rumours of a successful contract bid for another 263 Primary School Nativity Play souvenirs. Shares in T-Towel UK rose 36.7p as demand for biblical costumes soared with nearly £43 million changing hands over speculation of a 900p-a-share bid by blue-chip gainer Napkin Solutions, whose own shares hardened at 722¼ on news that takeover talks with French novelty headwear giants Cracahat had stalled. The biggest losers were Jojoba Industries with shares continuing to freefall on confirmation of news that they had lost another major Christmas cracker novelties contract to SuperKKX.

Shares at SuperKKX rose 1.25p to 1138¼ despite profit-takers moving in on the Yi Ylang Ylang-based blue-chip producer of blue-chips and other major choking hazards for 'Top Luxury Best Crackers'.

Technology

PS2, MP3, DAB, 3G, WAP, BMX, PSP (with gigabox). Gadgets, 'boys-toys' and technology generally has an annoying habit of using abbreviations that can add to confusion when sourcing Christmas presents (*see* **Choices**). Be particularly careful when asking an older person to buy technology for your present and if it cannot be avoided, ensure all details are written down clearly including the shop they have to get it from.

Hull schoolboy Paul Topping (14) made the mistake of asking his Nan for an MP3 (in white or silver) and received a Renault Scenic (in metallic cappuccino). Low mileage though.

He felt unable to say anything as she was already upset, not to mention confused, by the iPod Nano she'd received.

Things You Wouldn't Be Seen Dead In
(*See Novelty Socks; Novelty Slippers; Novelty Ties; Panto-mimes; Foot Spas; a Nissan Micra and so on*)

Tracy Island

A generation of parents was caught completely un-prepared by the Thunderbirds craze, particularly as the original TV show dated back to the late 1960s. The frenzied search for related merchandise became a pre-Christmas nightmare, and none more so than for Chingford hairdresser Tracy Island. 'It was terrible,' she recalled. 'My phone was ringing at all hours – I'd be half way through a light perm when the mobile would ring and it'd be some woman asking how much I wanted for it and did it come with Parker. In the end I went ex-directory and changed my name by deed poll,' recounted Miss Furby-Lightyear. (*See also 'Must-have' Toy*)

Tree

(*See 'Second Cowboy'*)

Trivial Pursuit, 'Cheeses'

(*See Board Games and Trivial Pursuit, 'Pies'; then throw a six for Trivial Pursuit – 'Pie' or 'Cheese'?*)

⚓ *Festive Focus on:*

Trivial Pursuit – 'Pie' or 'Cheese'?

Since the game's invention in the late 1970s, controversy has raged over what to call the little plastic triangle-shaped bits you slot into the 'wheels' of your playing piece when correctly answering a Trivial Pursuit 'pie'/'cheese' question.

A 1986 survey conducted by the Institute of Advanced Mathematics and Statistics at Lancaster University revealed a North/South divide with 56 per cent of UK residents living in the south of the country preferring 'cheese' and just 12 per cent using the term 'pie'. An overwhelming 268 per cent of UK residents in the north used 'pie' but only 84.72 per cent 'cheese'. The fascinating survey also revealed that a combination of regional dialects and family arguments had increased the possibility of the survey being completely useless by an overwhelming 76.3 per cent, representing a 52 per cent improvement on their survey about Druids.

In Italy, the preference is for '*Formaggio' di Insequimento Insignificante* (Trivial Pursuit 'Cheese') whilst the Dutch use *de Obelangrijke 'pastei' vand de Achtervolging* (Trivial Pursuit 'Pie'). The Germans' preference for 'pie' is fairly obvious and options include meat and potato or fruit.

A 1998 EU directive from Brussels (*don't see* **Overcooked Brussels Sprouts**) recommended use of the generic Euro word 'chezpai', to be phased in over a three-year period from 1 March 2002. The EU Trivial Pursuit Steering Committee discovered further popular alternatives such as 'cake' and 'wedge' which cast even more doubt over the validity of the 1986 Lancaster survey. The 1998 EU Repeal of the Trivial Pursuit Act followed, largely due to lobbying from the Monopoly Commission led by Colonel Mustard in the House of Lords with a candlestick.

Trivial Pursuit, 'Pies'

(*See* **Board Games** *and* **Trivial Pursuit, 'Cheeses'** *then answer a question on Art and Literature before moving one space to* **Trivial Pursuit – 'Pie' or 'Cheese'?**)

Turkey, Alternatives To

Greece is supposed to be similar and the people are equally friendly. Direct flights are available from most major UK airports.

Turkey, Another Alternative To

The common festive alternative to turkey is goose. However, great care should be taken in the preparation; simply suggesting 'shall we have a goose' can lead to a possible police caution and Asbo.

Turkey, Ordering

Forget the 'fresh versus frozen' debate or even the massive queues, there is a bigger obstacle to overcome when placing your order for the Christmas turkey.

The experience is not dissimilar to that of hiring a rental car for your holiday. The amount of passengers (plus luggage) need to fit into the vehicle you choose to hire. It's simple. That is until you get to the Rental desk.

Before you know it, your preference for a three-door 'mid-sized compact' has been upgraded into a 12-seater MPV with roof-rack.

And it's the same with the turkey, just substitute 'passengers' for family members/dinner guests, 'luggage' for appetite and it's virtually an identical scenario. All is clear in your mind as you join the queue. You need an 18 lb bird. Two hours later and you're leaving the order desk having been panicked into 'upgrading' to a 36 lb bird so big it'll need the oven doors removing just to get a leg in (*see* **Wedge**).

'Anybody else suddenly want to become a vegetarian?'

Twelfth Night

All Christmas decorations must be back in the loft by January the 6th. Or the bogeyman gets you. Don't believe it, huh? Did you say 'Candyman' five times in front of the mirror? Did you walk under that ladder? No, I didn't think so. Well it's the same thing. So just get everything back in the loft by the twelfth night. The clock is ticking.

Twindows

The final double doors on an advent calendar, which, when opened, reveal the largest piece of chocolate (*see Advent Calendars*).

Unwanted Presents

Unwanted presents can enhance the whole giving and receiving experience. An unwanted present you receive can be passed on the following year making it a more pleasurable 'win-win' result. Avoid all embarrassment in giving the same present back to the same person by just checking in advance e.g. 'What did you give me last Christmas?' (*See also Keep Your Receipt*)

'How ingenious! A matching tie and kimono set! Why that'll be simply perfect for re-wrapping and giving to my brother-in-law next Christmas.'

Unwanted Visitors

(*See **Mulled Wine***)

🍮 🍮 🍮 🍮 🍮 🍮 🍮 🍮 🍮 🍮 🍮 🍮 🍮 🍮 🍮 🍮 🍮

Wedge

(*See **Cake, Trivial Pursuit – 'Pie' or 'Cheese'** and see, I told you that turkey wouldn't fit in the oven*)

White Christmas, Betting on

An 'official' White Christmas is when one snowflake falls on the roof of the Weather Centre in London. So it's no good trudging through 4-metre deep drifts on your way to collect your winnings from Ladbrokes if it doesn't happen to be snowing in London.

The last recorded 'official' White Christmas was in 1973, the year before a 50,000 megawatt industrial turbo-convector heater was installed on the roof of the London Weather Centre.

(*See also* **Christmas Number 1s**)

🍮 🍮 🍮 🍮 🍮 🍮 🍮 🍮 🍮 🍮 🍮 🍮 🍮 🍮 🍮 🍮

Yi Ylang Ylang

A small industrial town in northern China, which since 1994 has taken over from Jojoba in Taiwan, to become the world's leading manufacturer, producing 93 per cent of all plastic novelties found in Christmas crackers. A staggering 5.7 billion plastic hairslides, brooches, toy cars, dice, puzzles, yo-yos, frogs, keyrings, cowboys and other choking hazards are produced each year and exported for use in 'Top Luxury Best Crackers' and other well-known cracker ranges.

Zulu

Amongst the Christmas TV schedules will be a selection described as 'all-time movie classics'. We know these as 'repeats'. To establish the most repeated 'all-time movie classic', it seemed a sensible idea, at the time, to ask the opinion of Edith Grainger (89), resident of the 'Greenacres' Nursing Home for the Infirm and Elderly in Winchester.

Mrs Grainger has done nothing but watch the telly since arriving at 'Greenacres' sixty-two years ago and amazes fellow residents with her expansive knowledge of TV scheduling – particularly over the Christmas period:

That *Zulu* with Michael Whatsisname and Dale Winton is the one that always comes up. Always. But, do you know, I never enjoyed it more than when it was repeated for the seventeenth time back in 1989. Or was it 1889? The scenery and colour! It was marvellous, dear. You see, they were doing a Michael Caine double-bill and *Jaws 3* was on before *Zulu* and I still had my 3-D glasses on.

Acknowledgements

To everybody who contributed, knowingly or otherwise.

Thanks to Dave Burt, Jon Butler (for putting up with Mariah), all Power-Lunch Club Members, Stef Bierwerth, Jacqui Butler, Oliver Clarke and to Charlotte, for sharing my sense of humour.

To the exclusive member of my Power-Breakfast Club, thanks for the support and encouragement over the years.